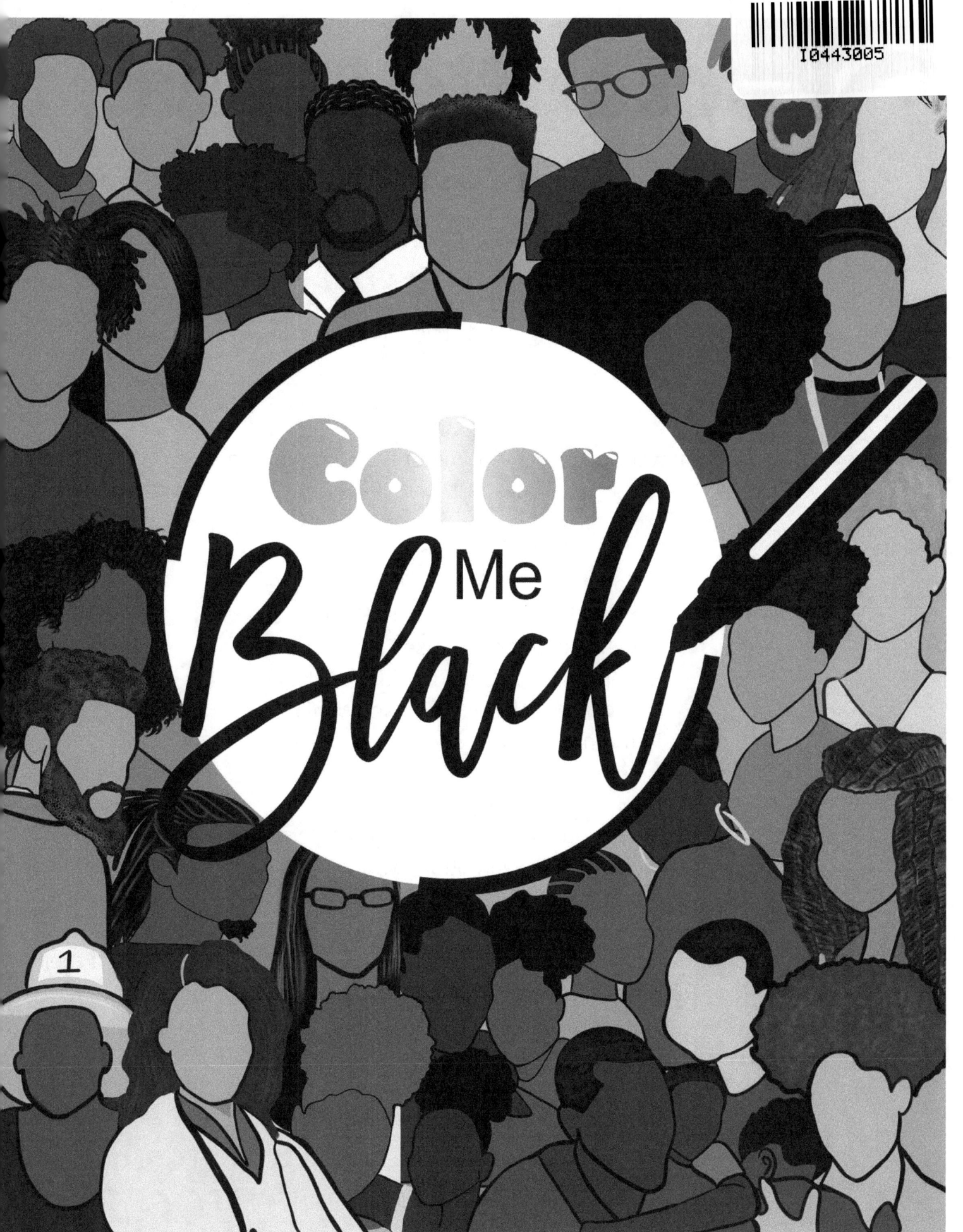

# Color Me Black

## Mission:

To provide the community with the empowering tool of
art therapy to help facilitate healing and joy. We want to remind the minority
community of its abundance and value to this world through this visual
showcasing of positive affirmations.

## Vision:

To empower and enrich the minority community through
art.

## Declaration:
Color Me Black because I am STRONG
Color Me Black because I am BEAUTIFUL
Color Me Black because I am SMART
Color Me Black because I am VALUED
Color Me Black because I am WORTHY
Remember to always color me…BLACK

## Juneteenth:
Two and a half years after President
Lincoln's Emancipation Proclamation - which had become official
January 1, 1863. On June 19, 1865, about two months after the Confederate
General Robert E. Lee surrendered at Appomattox, VA., Union General Gordon
Granger arrived in Galveston, Texas, to inform enslaved African-Americans of their
freedom and that the Civil War had ended.

June 19, 1863 is our Independence Day! So as a
dedication to freedom, the Color Me Black coloring books will give you nineteen
coloring pages of cultural manifestation.

By: Shyle Woods

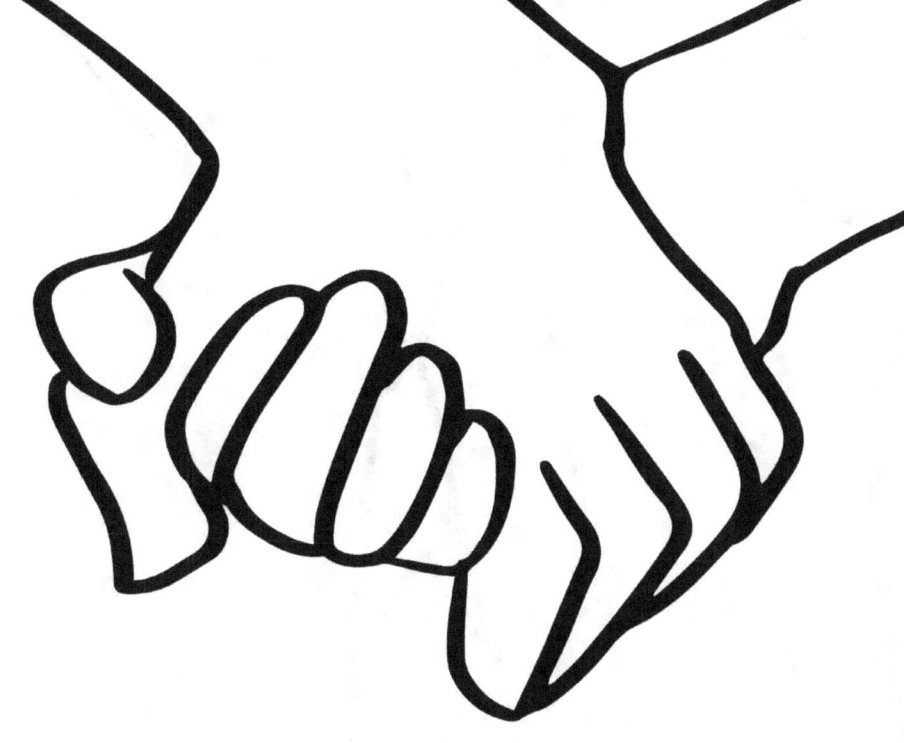

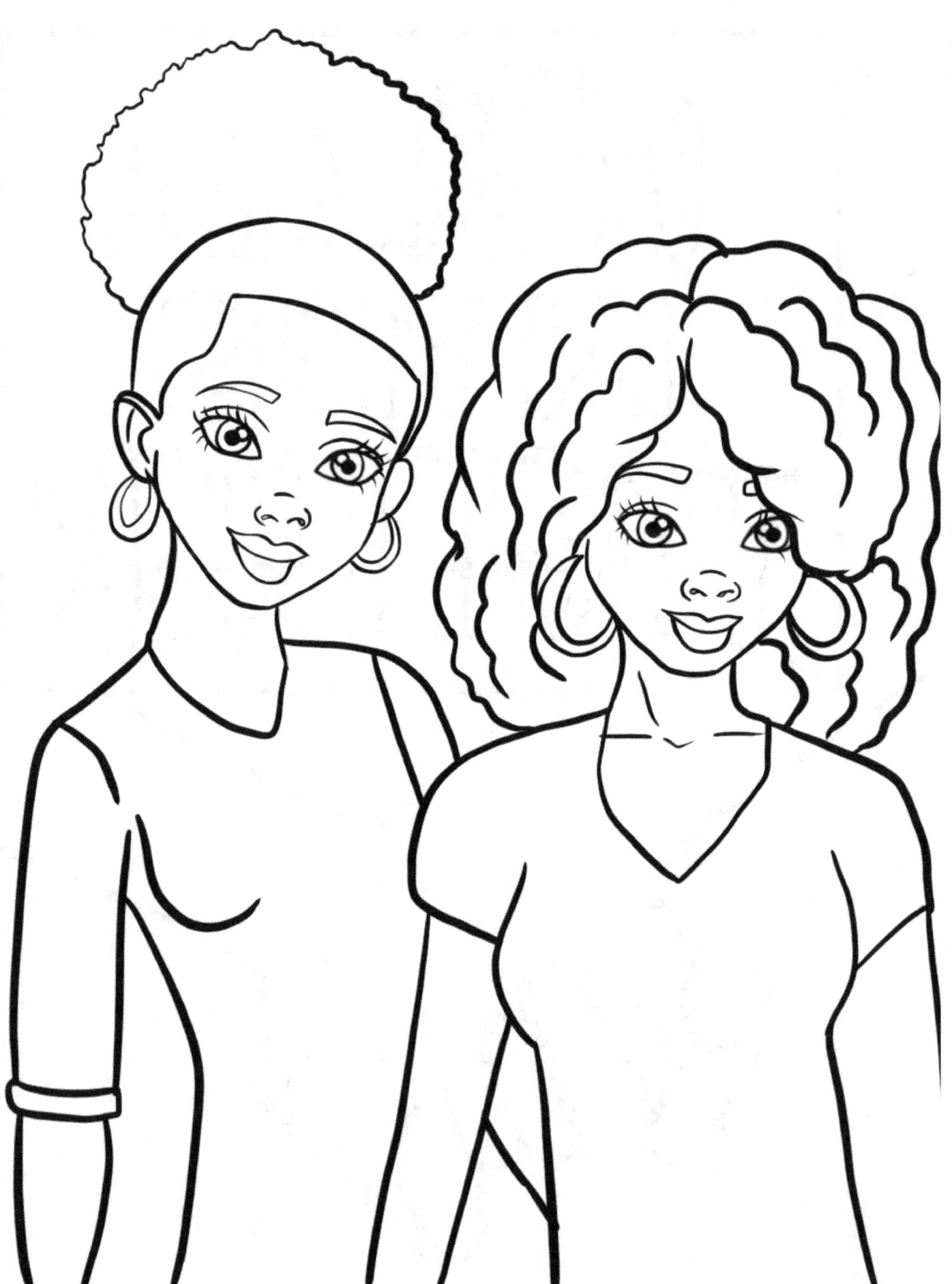

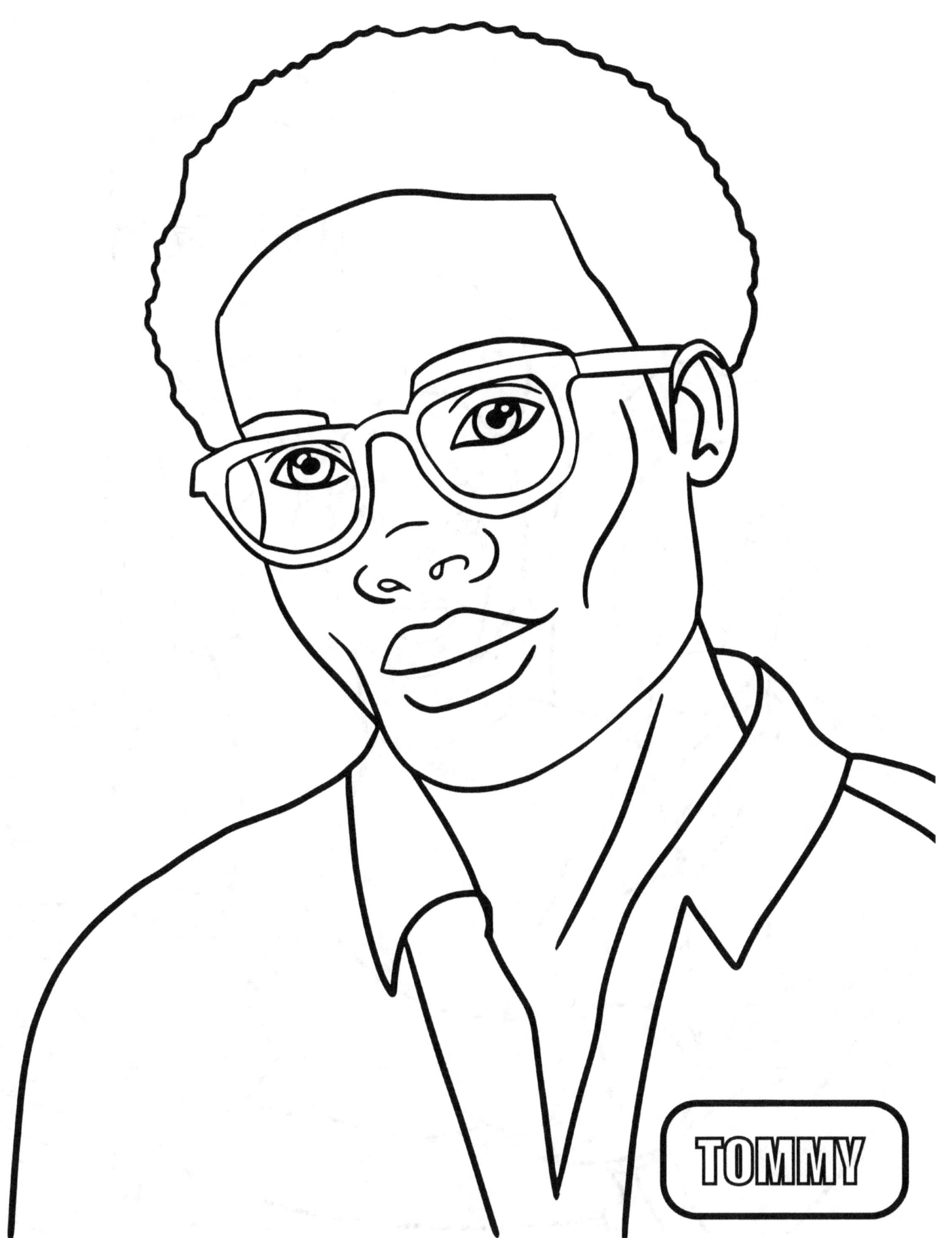

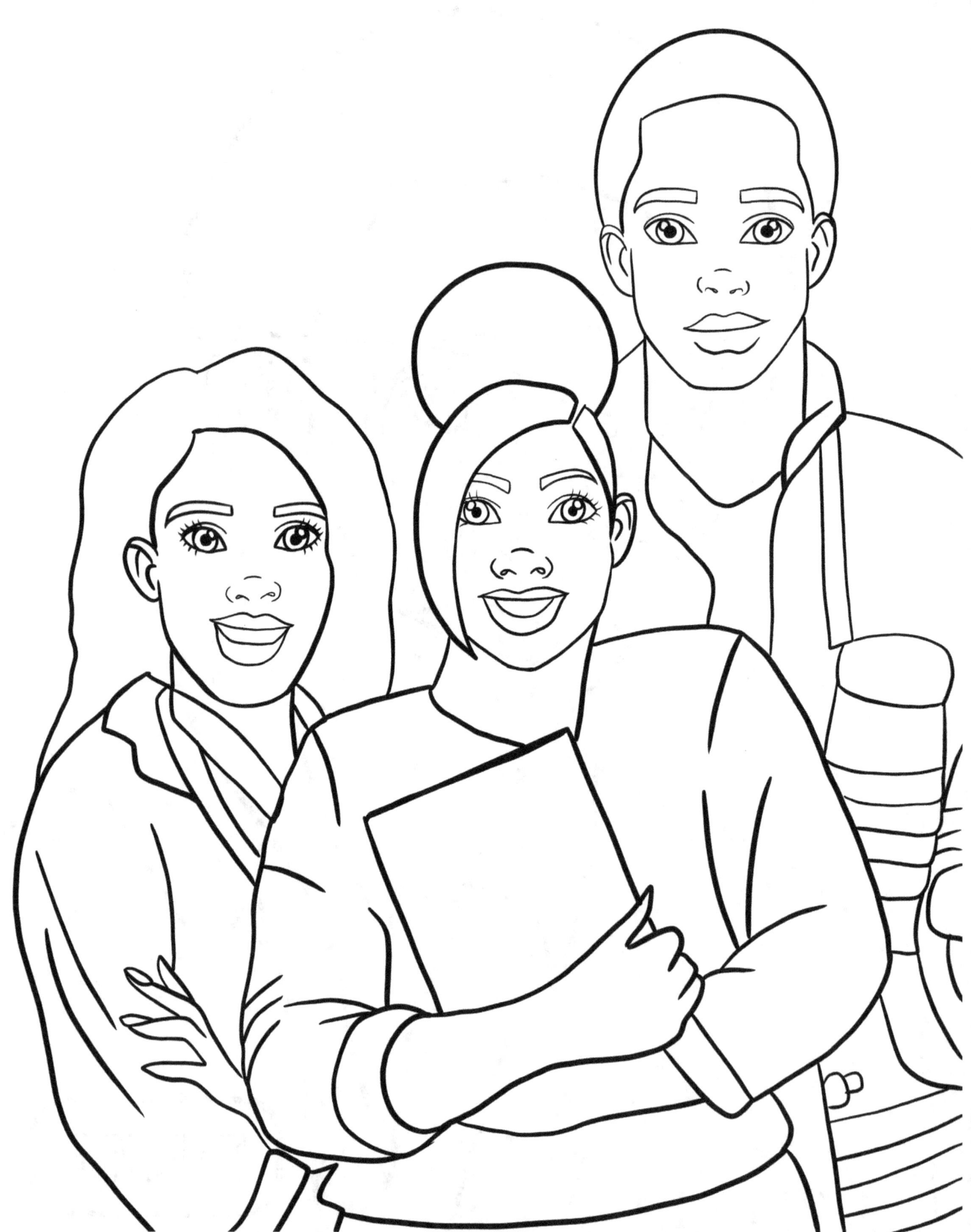

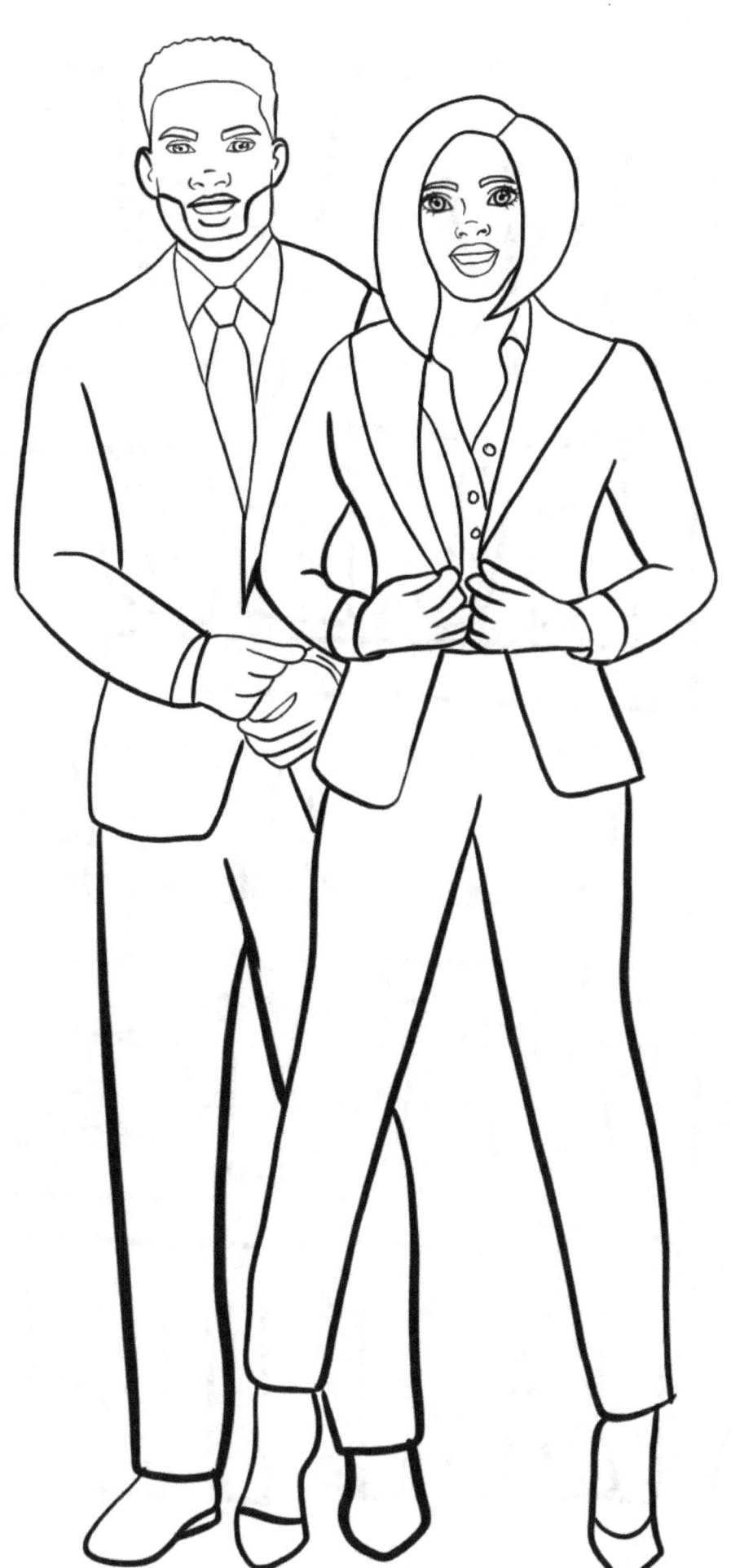

# BLACK LIVES DREAMS & FUTURE MATTER

1 2 3 4 5 6 7 8 9 10

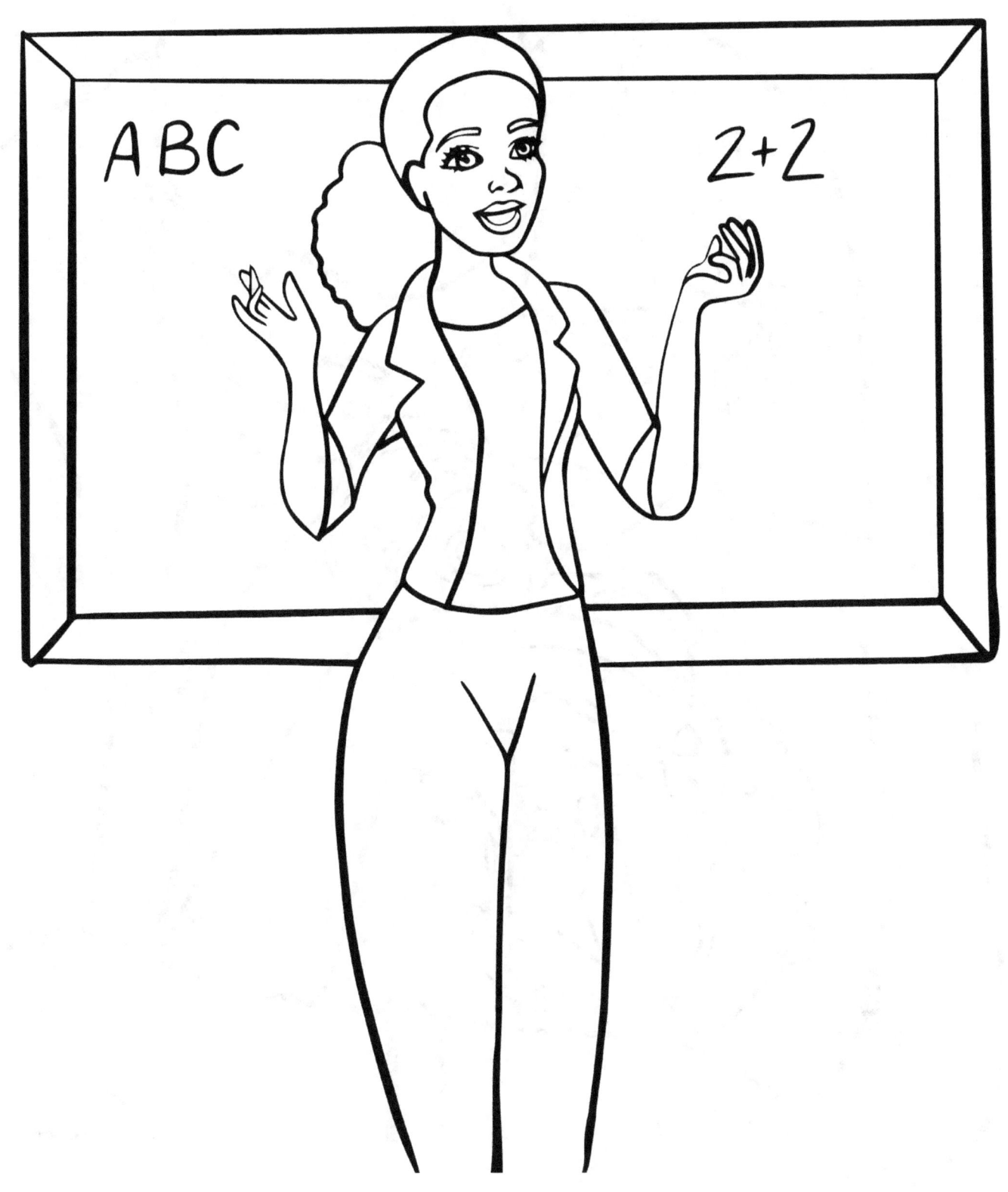

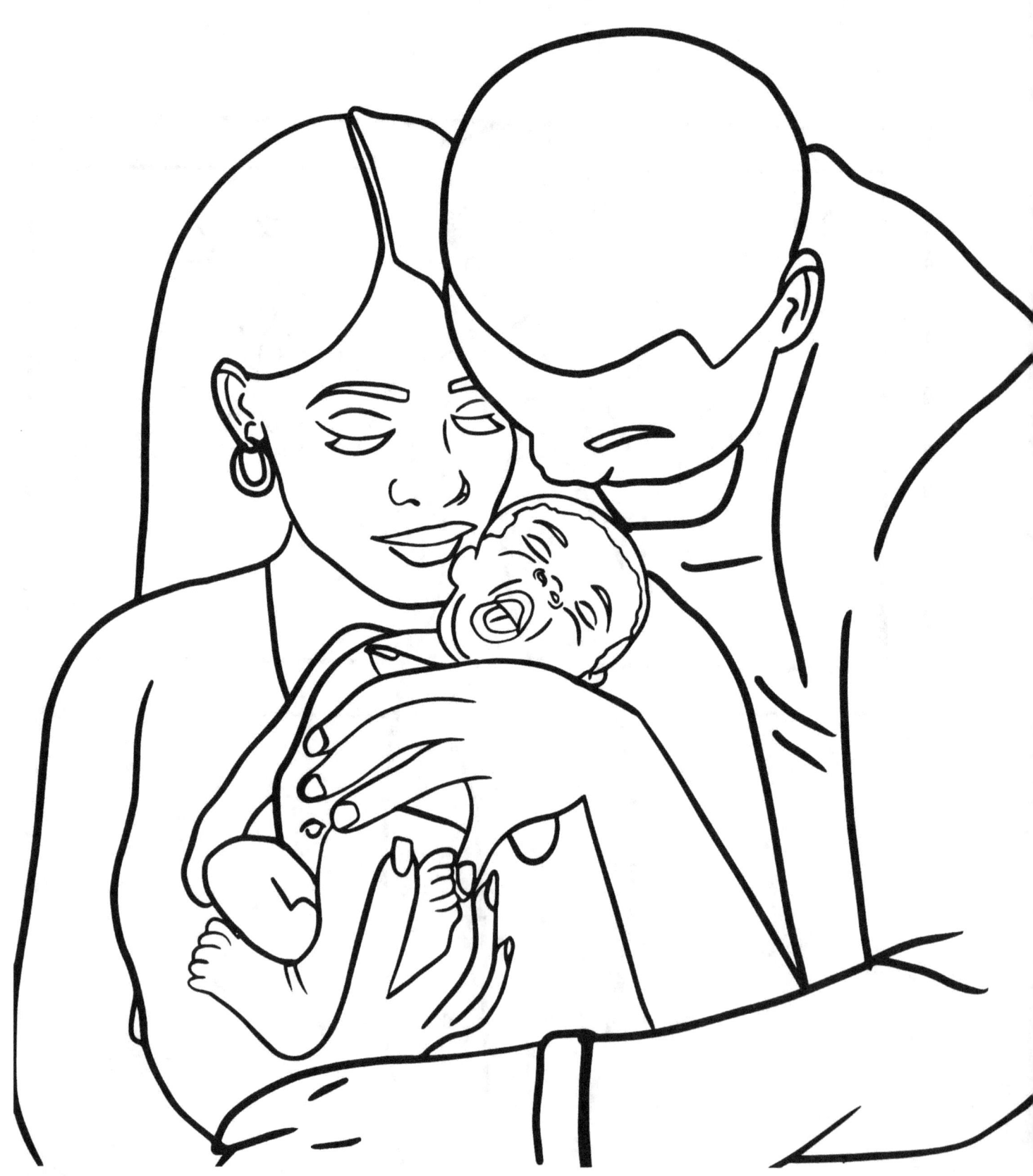

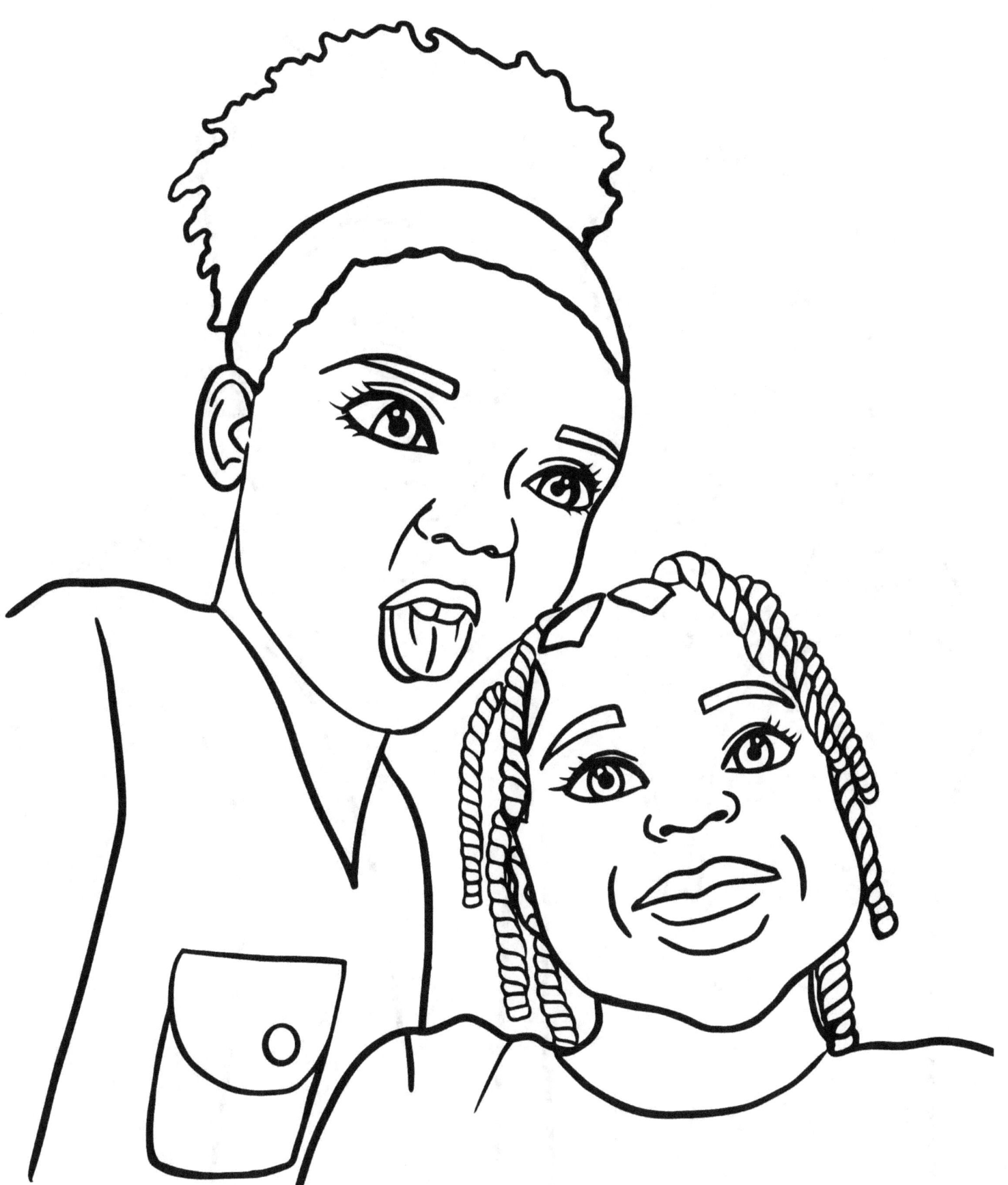

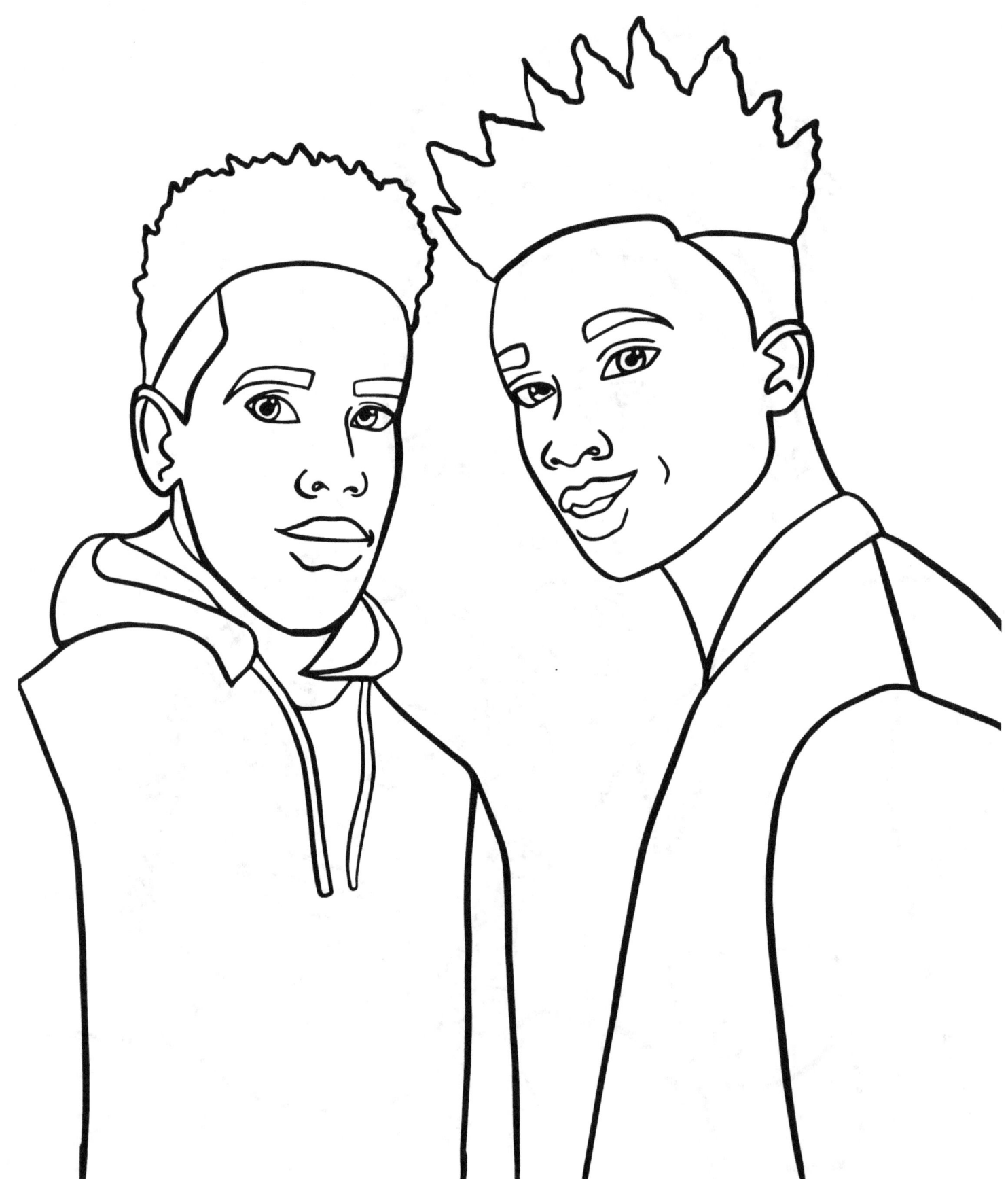

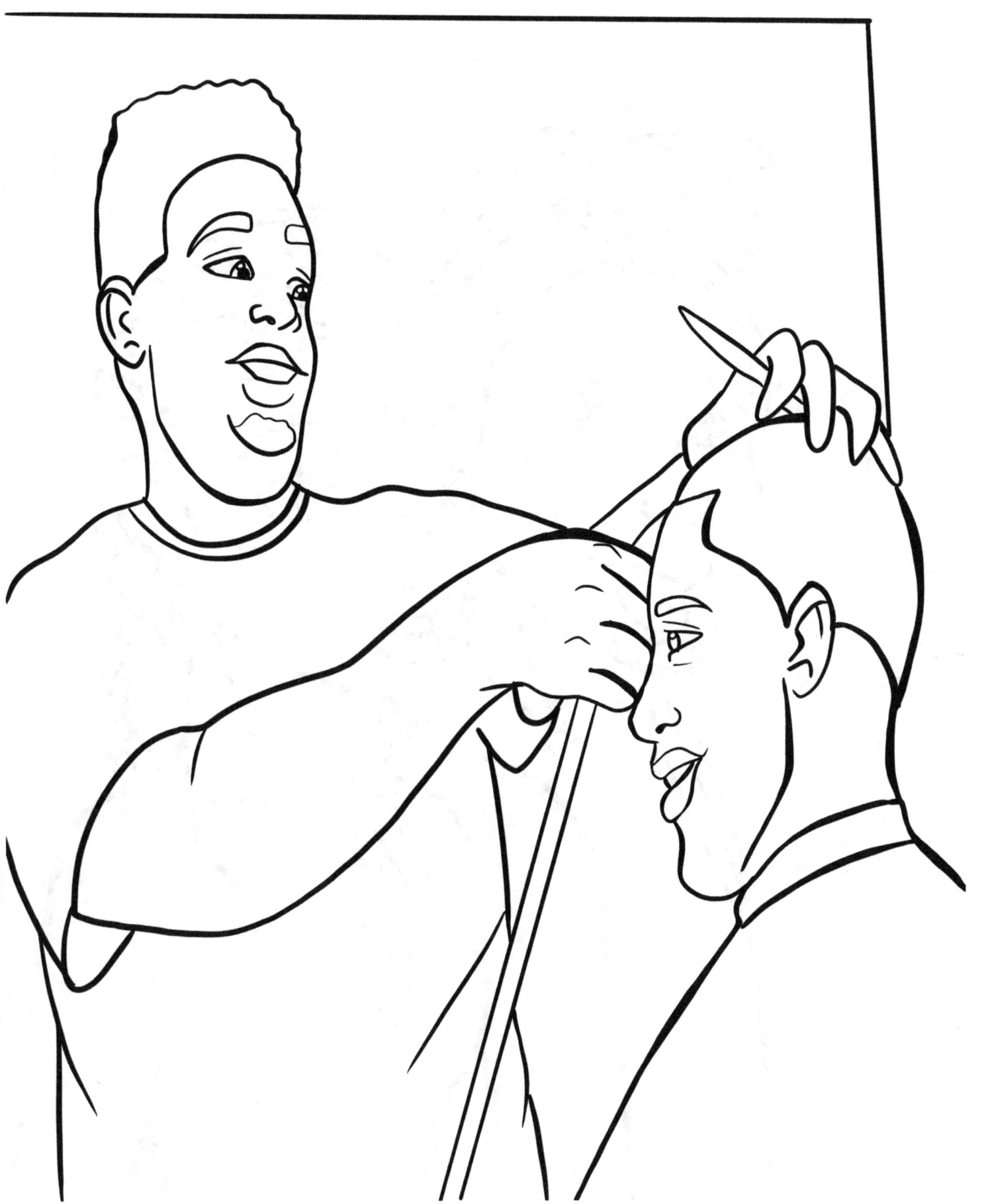

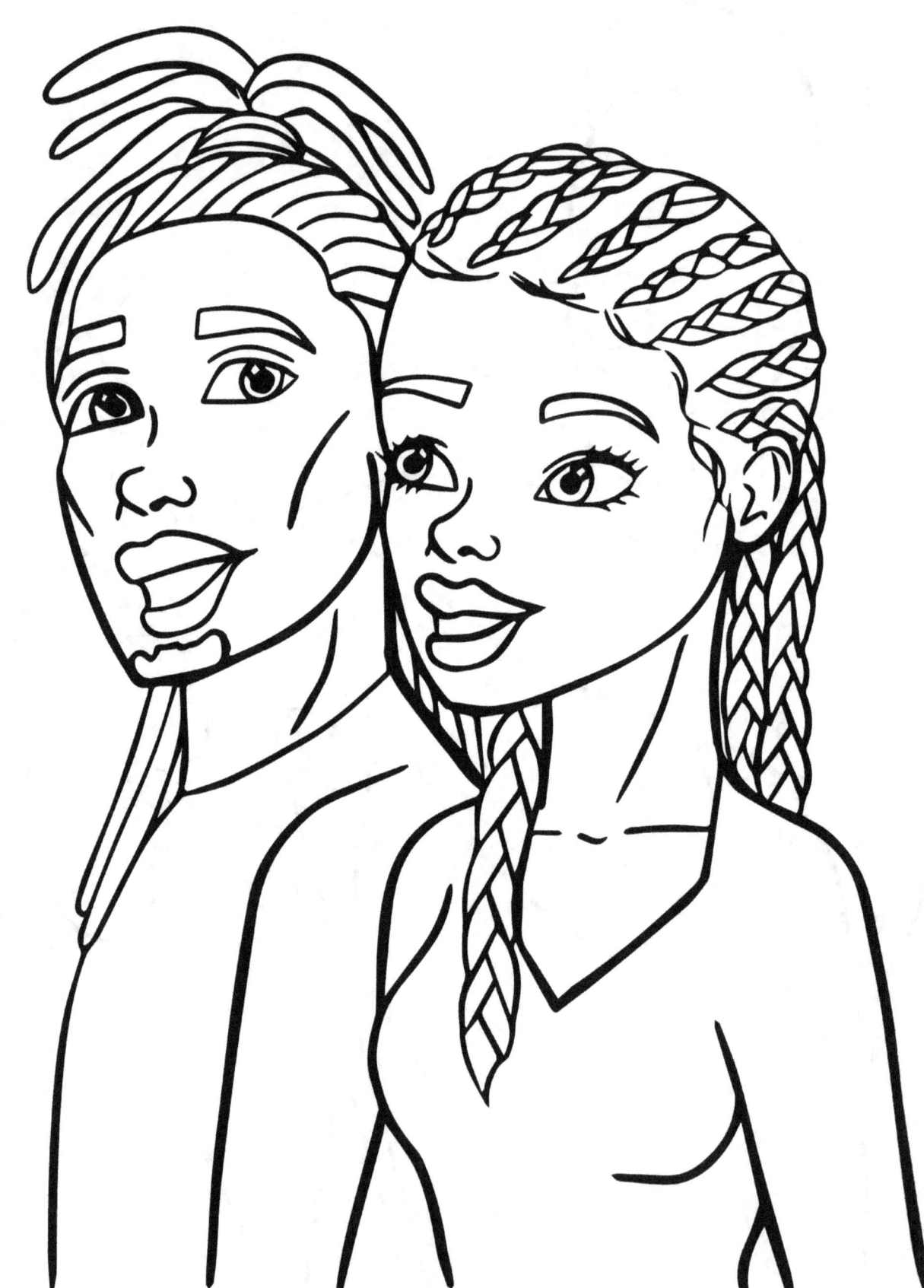

- LISTEN
- HAVE Empathy
- BLACK LIVES MATTER
- Talk about The Tough Stuff

# JOY

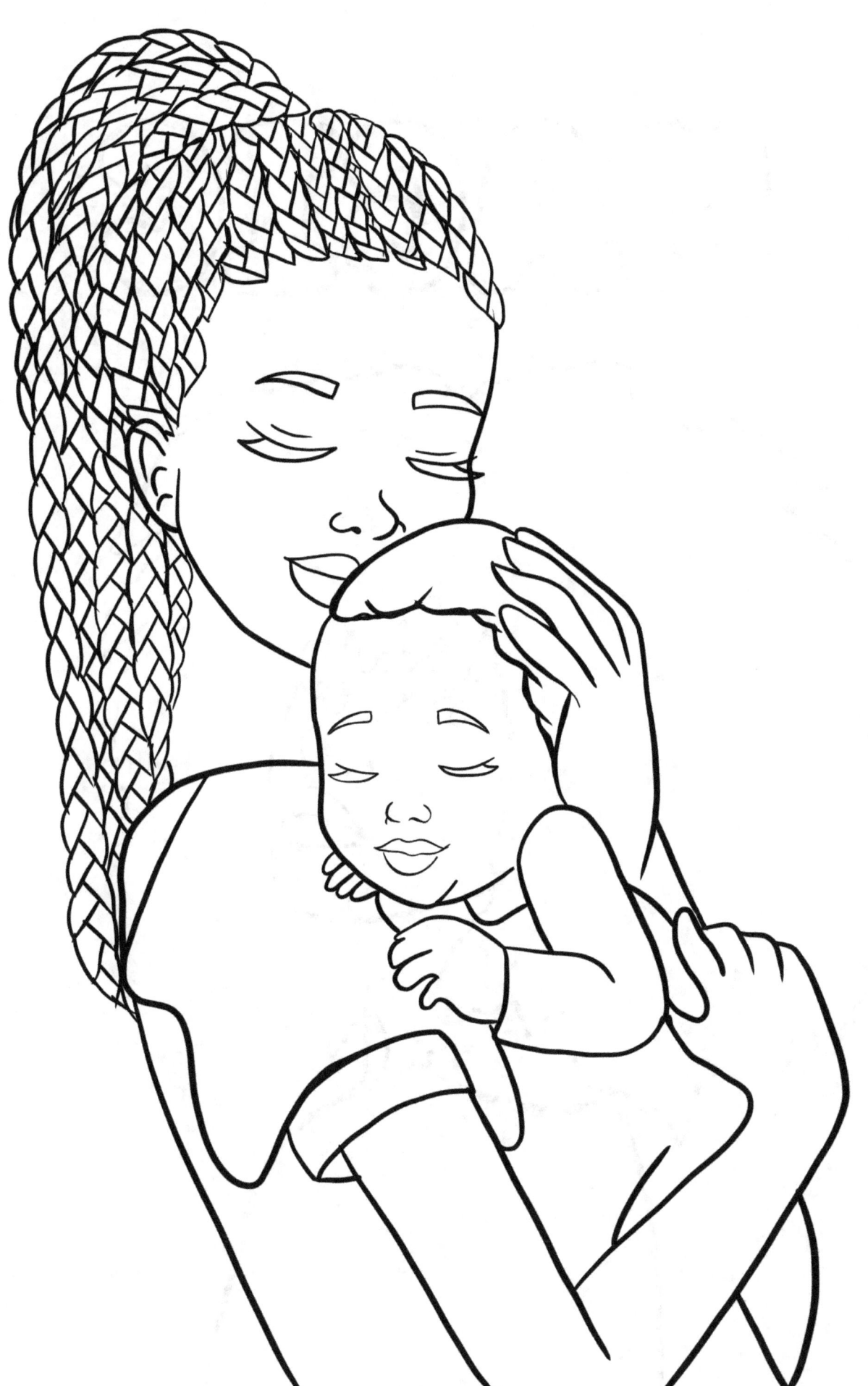

# MAGIC

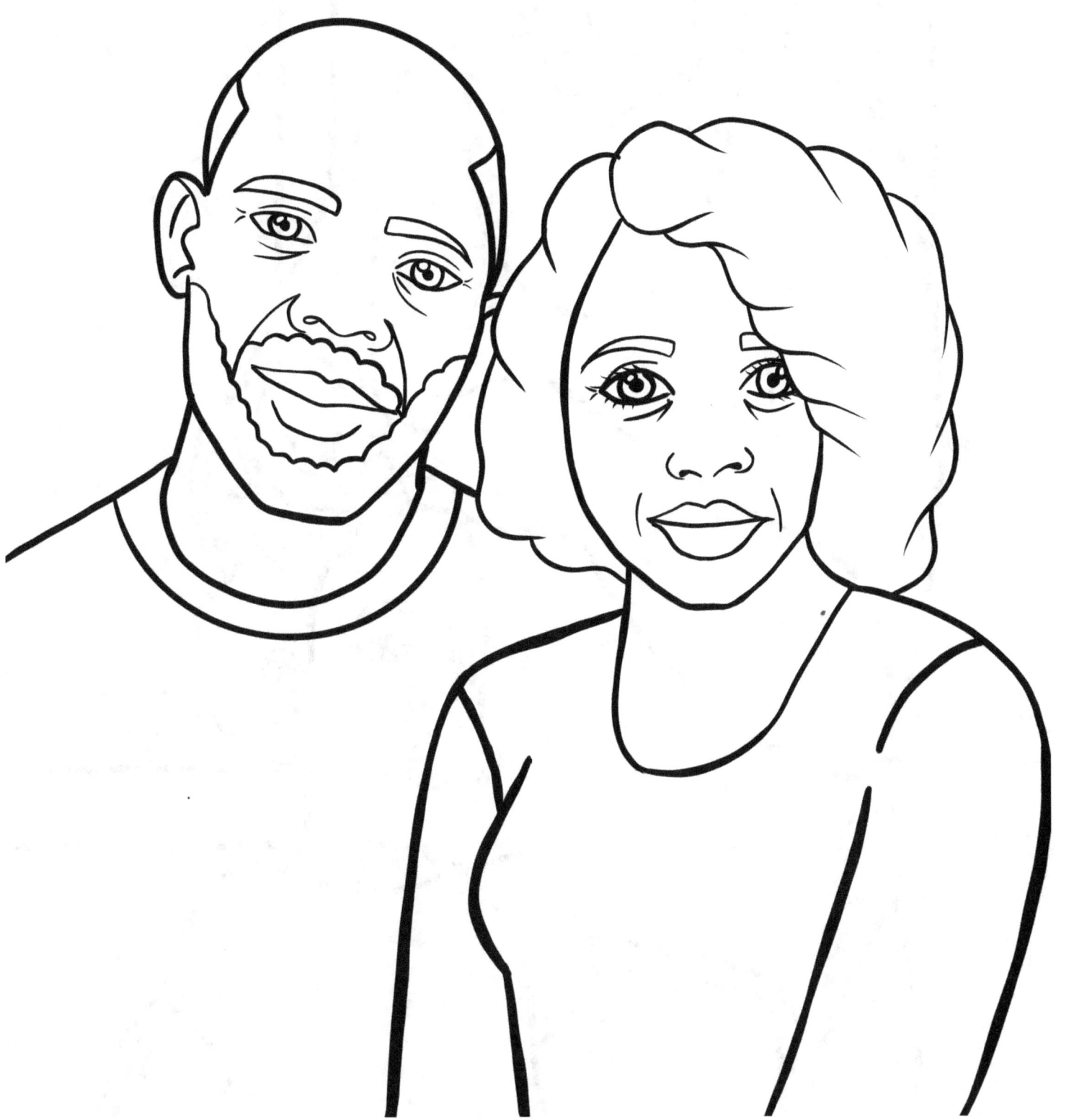

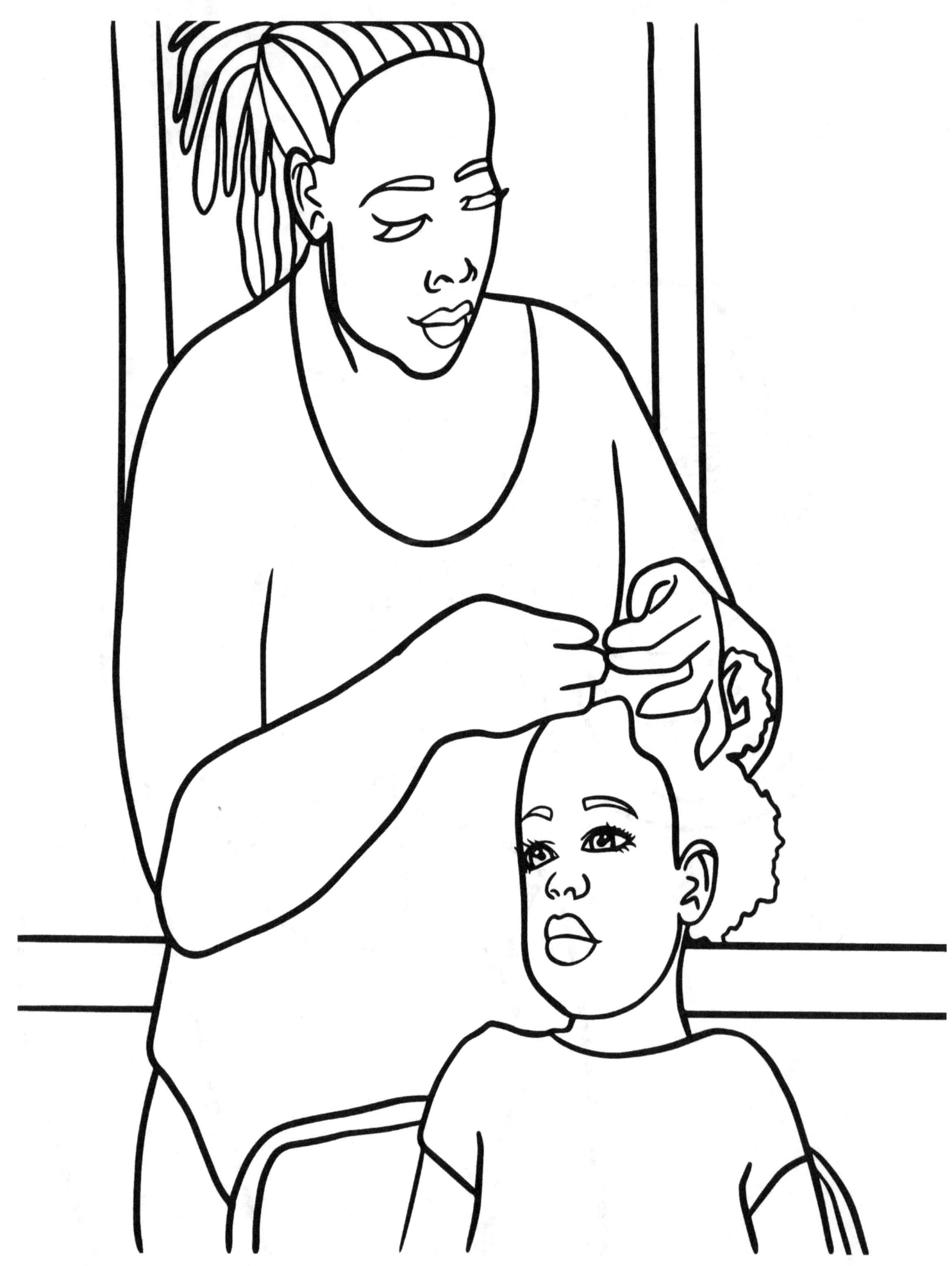

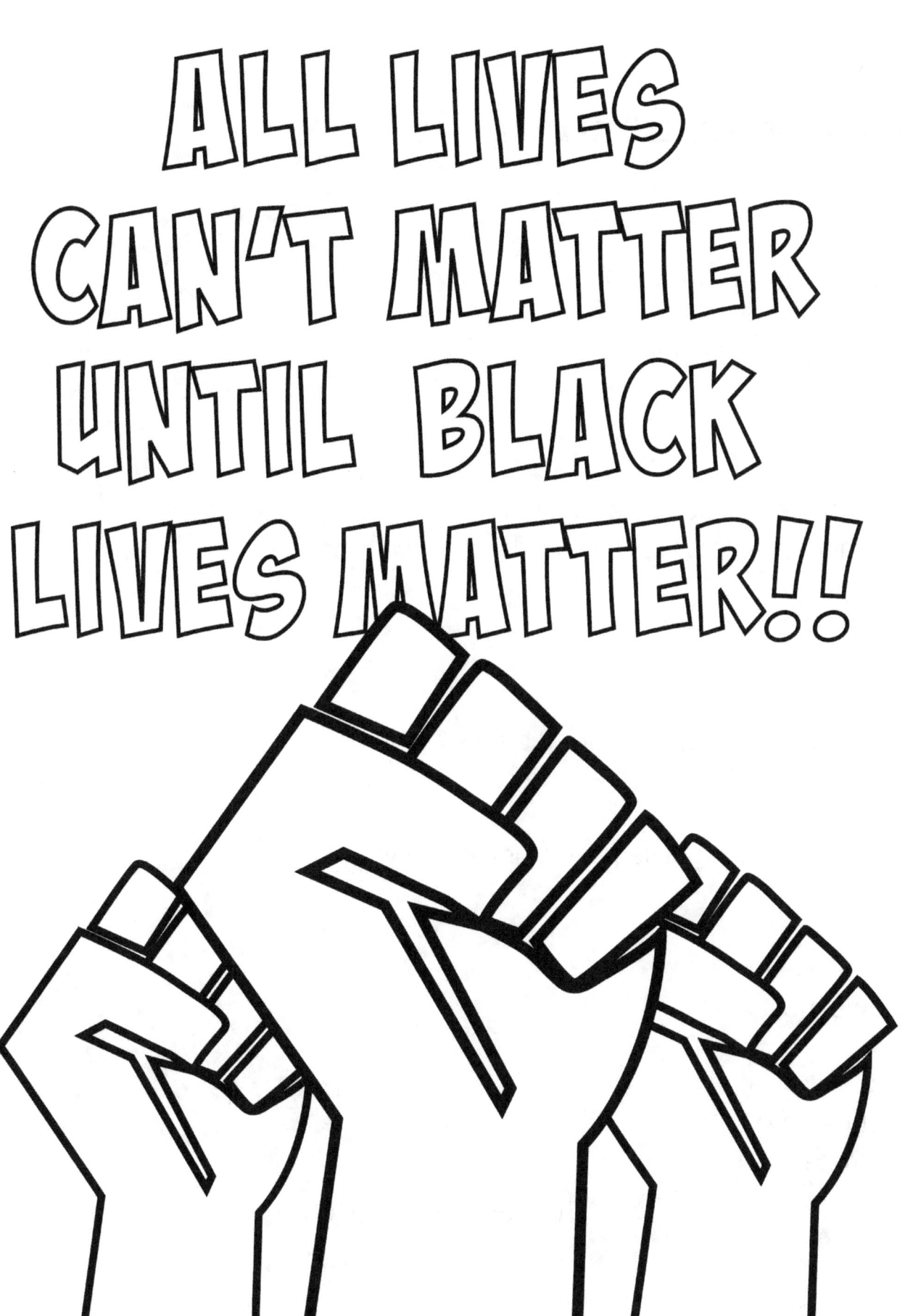

## **Official Juneteenth Poem**

We Rose

From Africa's heart, we rose

Already a people, our faces ebon, our bodies lean,

We rose

Skills of art, life, beauty and family
Crushed by forces we knew nothing of, we rose

Survive we must, we did,
We rose

We rose to be you, we rose to be me,
Above everything expected, we rose

To become the knowledge we never knew,
We rose

Dream, we did
Act we must


Kristina Kay,
We Rose © 1996,

Juneteenth.com

**What makes you strong?**

**What makes you feel beautiful?**

**What makes you smart?**

**What makes you feel valuable?**

**What makes you feel worthy?**

**Why do I like being black?**

_____
_____
_____
_____
_____
_____
_____
_____
_____
_____
_____
_____
_____
_____
_____
_____
_____
_____
_____
_____
_____
_____
_____
_____
_____
_____
_____

www.ingramcontent.com/pod-product-compliance
Lightning Source LLC
Chambersburg PA
CBHW080819220526

45466CB00011BB/3619